The Comedy of Agony

Also by Christopher Spranger

The Effort to Fall, 1998, Green Integer

The Book of Tasks: Volume I: Atlantean Undertakings, 2022, Coyote Arts

The Comedy of Agony

of

A Book of Poisonous Contemplations

Christopher Spranger

COYOTE ARTS

Albuquerque : 2023

The Comedy of Agony © 2006, 2023 Christopher Spranger.

All rights reserved. No portion of this book may be reproduced in any manner or placed in an electronic retrieval system without the express written permission of the author and the publisher, except for short excerpts used in reviews.

Book design by Jordan Jones. Cover design by Linda Zupcic. Cover illustration: *Hölle*, from the *Hortus Deliciarum*, Hohenbourg.

ISBN: 978-1-58775-039-7 (paper)
ISBN: 978-1-58775-040-3 (e-book)
Library of Congress Control Number: 2023930143

Second edition. Previously: Leaping Dog Press Book #12.

Coyote Arts LLC
Jordan Jones, Editor and Co-Publisher
PO Box 6690
Albuquerque, New Mexico 87197-6690
USA

SAN 254-0126

Coyote Arts LLC

www.coyote-arts.com

Contents

Book the First

I. La Dolorosa Scienza.. 15
II. Predicament and Impasse.. 37
III. A Few Twirls Around the Tomb................................ 57

Book the Second

Diabolical Fidelity.. 81
The Genealogy of Denial... 87
The Worst Wait... 89
The Unenlightened.. 91
Laughter and Logic.. 94
The Infernal Lure.. 96
Stoicism's Mistake... 100
Where God and Man Meet... 102
Termite as Exemplar.. 103
Ave Caesar!.. 105
Social Convenience of the False Concept................... 107
The Attractions of Rage... 109
River and Whirlpool.. 111
Omnia Amor Vincit.. 112
New Enemies... 113
Suicide, Virginity, and Tears...................................... 115
Rise of the Pharmaceutical... 117
The Last Prophet... 120
Entrenched In Time... 123
The Perversion of Compassion................................... 125
The Buddhist Hell... 127
Time and Vitality... 131
From Starlight to Electric Light................................. 133
The Portioning Out of Eyes....................................... 135
La Scienza Nuova.. 137
The Unconquerable?.. 139

Book the First

I.
La Dolorosa Scienza

In the drama of the spirit, as in that of the body, it is Pain that plays the hero's role.

*

The earth is all conceivable pain compacted into a single point.

*

Only because they fall silently are teardrops so freely indulged. Were their descent made *audible,* the desperate would no longer permit themselves to weep, for fear of blowing out their neighbors' eardrums.

*

A tender heart, like a rotted tooth, needs to be kept numb, if one is going to make it through this painful procedure called life without continually screaming.

*

Chances are pretty good we're in the presence of Truth if we begin shivering uncontrollably. When attempting to sift the Real from the merely philosophical, let gooseflesh be your guide.

*

A mental and emotional bulimic, the thinker wolfs down perplexities, doubts, disappointments, stuffs himself full of pain and misfortune. Then back out it all comes, in the form of a "philosophical work."

*

All is air — and we, the heirs of air.

*

History? A complete blank. Only what happens in the heart and cannot be recorded has *content.*

*

The brain is by far the stupidest part of man's being, but it is base and bold enough to present itself as a great pioneer, and lives lavishly on the praise procured for it by this false appearance.

That a higher concentration of knowledge is to be found in the heart than in any other bodily organ, including the brain, is borne out by the fact that it *constantly bleeds*. Something like a hemorrhage would be required to catapult the brain to the heart's level.

*

The heart, once conquered by love, is about as reliable a guide as candlelight in a hurricane.

*

All the great creators have been plagiarists of incredible boldness, beginning with God, Who has made not the feeblest effort to conceal the fact He ripped off the idea for this universe from the Devil.

*

If the purpose of art is to help us understand the pain of life, then the purpose of life must be to multiply our pains, so that we may better appreciate the power of art.

*

The philosophers and religious teachers of the past labored under the delusion that what man needed was *meaning,* and each tried, in his own way, to fill the void. Fortunately today's mercantile societies have emancipated us from this false notion, demonstrating that what man in fact needs are five days a week of pointless tasks, followed by two of pointless entertainment. Nothing satisfies him less than having a *soul.*

*

When wounded, an animal yelps or howls aloud. Whereas that victim of civilization and snob of pain, the poet, turning up his nose at these passé genres, proudly grips his pen. — Writing? A pretentious form of howling.

*

Our moments of delight always come back to haunt us. Maybe that's the only reason they come at all.

*

The pains I'm most impressed by and never tire of contemplating are those that can't be *pinned down.* Take, for example, this dull yet sharp, pulsing yet unceasing pain I feel right now. Below the ribs on my right side is where

I'd like to locate it, but is it really there? Like a nervous bird it takes wing every time I fix my attention on the spot from which it seems to emanate. When I'm still, it's still, and when I move, it moves, as if it were making sport of me. Where does this mysterious pain come from? What drew it here, and where is it headed?

*

Every great metropolis is a garbage disposal for human dreams.

*

Nature was lost in a dream that must have lasted millions of years; then in waltzed man, accompanied by a chorus of jackhammers, and woke her up.

*

Every scream is an attempt by the nerves to *name* a sensation.

*

In the landscape of the emotions, sorrow is a mountain, and joy, a cloud.

*

He claims to have been touched by happiness and hasn't a single scar to prove it.

*

An inclination to reflection spoils everything. Could fruit reflect it would rot on the tree before even becoming ripe.

*

More than a philosophical position, nihilism is a method of self-defense adopted by men who, knowing a little too well what knowledge is, where it leads, and what it does, *fear* it.

*

The greatest pains wound you in some part of yourself you weren't even aware existed.

*

We only succeed in eluding despair in proportion as we succeed in eluding ourselves.

*

I don't want illusion in my life — no, not even the merest wisp of it. I would much rather have reality in all of its terrible realness turned up a hundred degrees.

*

There is no scream of horror that could not be mistaken for an *exact description* of the universe.

*

If the way to the highest spirituality be through the intensest reality, then there are few things in life more spiritual than *physical* pain.

*

The most fascinating physical pains are akin to emotional and spiritual ones in that they completely elude our grasp. They are masters of the shifty maneuver — far too fugitive to put a finger on. Unlike those pains which plant themselves in a particular place, which find a favorite spot and settle down, these remain phantasmally elusive. They wander in one day without being announced and depart on the next without a proper goodbye.

*

Nobody but God has the right to be lonelier and more irresponsible than a poet.

*

The headache is Nature's none too subtle way of informing the man unaccustomed to reflect of what having a brain *feels like*.

*

What a lesson in humility is in store for the Scream on the day when the Teardrop discovers her voice!

*

Bad luck can't be learnt or acquired: it takes genius. In fact genius itself is a form of bad luck. The *ultimate* form.

*

Every heartache has roots which plunge down to the very deepest level of God's utter indifference to human pain.

*

The heart? A towering pile of fireworks into which Love, looking bored, flings a match.

*

Loneliness does not permeate the heart, it supplants it. Blood permeates the heart, but loneliness supplants that too. In fact loneliness supplants one's entire being. Under the influence of loneliness, one's flesh and blood become *pure feeling*. They cease to be physical and become emotional; they turn from a limited presence into broadening absence. After welling up in the heart, loneliness spreads outwards like a dissolving mist and vaporizes one's entire being. And from there it proceeds to vaporize the entire universe around one, drawing it into the same abyss as one's being, where it dissolves and vanishes. To be lonely is to breathe loneliness in and to bleed loneliness out, until nothing more is left of oneself or anything else.

*

The most precious possession any person can have is the ability to delude himself.

*

Upon the tongue of the man whose sight is true lies the sum total of things intolerable to hear.

*

From Boredom's point of view, every blister is a miracle.

*

A tender look has the same effect on a sensitive heart as a tornado does on a haystack.

*

If misery be a mission, then everything which has ever been born into this world has had the same one.

*

"What purpose do all the pains and disappointments of life serve?" As a matter of fact, they don't serve any purpose. They *are* the purpose.

*

A teardrop is a temple erected by the heart in honor of trauma.

*

Smiles determined to rival each other in wideness fling themselves tauntingly at wounds that won't heal, so that these latter become embarrassed by their own existence and *bleed for shame.*

*

Only in our most violent fits of self-loathing do we get a glimpse of what it must feel like to be God.

*

Melancholy, theophany — what's the difference? You don't slide too far into sadness before hitting God head-on.

*

Obsessive thinking is the mind's version of internal bleeding.

*

We are accustomed to talk about catastrophe as if it were an unwelcome guest and not a secretly wished-for deliverance from the tedium of life.

*

A life without suffering belongs to the same order of ideas as a soup without broth.

*

At its apex, torment justifies — a religious man might even say, *sanctifies* — everything. So it is only right that Law, Golden Rule, and Categorical Imperative should doff their hats in the presence of a desperate man.

*

A sinking ship is usually abandoned. Then there's Love: the one we board.

*

An abiding desire to make oneself and someone else miserable is the only way to account for the continued existence of most relationships.

*

Good Fortune, being light-footed, goes fast away.

*

Have a look down that corridor from which your delights now come, and behold, following close on their heels, your future hardships.

*

How perverse to assign pain a beneficent purpose in the economy and maintenance of life! — to ceaselessly harp, as physicians do, on the dubious idea that pain is meant to alert us to some impending danger, thereby enabling us to protect ourselves against it. As if the majority of such alerts were not false alarms, and as if the rest were not grossly exaggerated. As if the sole purpose — so obscenely obvious — of pain, were not simply to make us *suffer!*

*

Of all we feel, only the pain is real. So why then do we seek to experience sensations of another kind? — or rather, hoodwink ourselves into believing that, as a matter of fact, we have?

*

Every shudder of delight is but a nervous breakdown *deferred*.

*

Sometimes life offers us what we desire most — as the desert does a mirage.

*

Pierced in its tenderest spot, cynicism bleeds moonlight.

*

An illusion is a bridge of lace stretched over the abyss.

*

To endure a solitary destiny, one must sometimes forget he isn't God.

*

The fittingest time for tragedy to befall a man is when he has suffered himself to forget Fiasco's dominance and begun to believe once again in the possibility of good fortune. For whatever exists must "correct" itself: our biography as much as the stock market. And this world having been created principally for the purpose of multiplying screams, it goes without saying that the *correct* state of anything is the one likeliest to bring to light the latent virtuosity of our vocal cords.

*

So good are the wealthy at spreading nothingness around themselves that one sometimes wonders if they aren't the world's single greatest source of it.

*

The most deeply wounded do not necessarily howl the loudest. Sometimes they barely whisper. And then, there are always a few extravagant enough to *sing*.

*

Far from being stricken by diseases, the body *accumulates* them. It is a collector of the Incurable.

*

Sickness is both a misfortune and a refuge.

*

There is a subtle but important difference between the insomniac and the man who has *conquered* sleep.

*

Knowledge being what it is, it's no wonder each man aspires to be a mystery to himself.

*

What is left after love ends? — Not even the illusion it existed.

*

The writer is more vulgar than the tormented do-nothing, because rather than honoring the nobility of his pain, he *puts it to work*. By exploiting it, he degrades it, and, in consequence, degrades himself: a shady business man bent on squeezing the maximum profit out of his every misfortune.

*

This world abounds in people like grass — born to be trampled.

*

A fresh wound always affords a thrill, no matter how many times we've been struck before. Bleeding is never *boring*.

*

Were sighing declared forbidden, I would explode into pieces within the space of an hour.

*

We human beings, like our canine friends, are never so content as when gnawing on a bone. Though it has been observed our finickier nature requires, to obtain genuine satisfaction, the bones of our own kind.

*

Man might be an autoimmune disease of Nature.

*

The Worst sometimes fails to happen of its own; being aware of this, God created man — to *make* it happen.

*

Nothing puts us into such a huff as hearing someone call into question the reality of our suffering. And understandably so. For, in the end, what else do we have?

*

Provided the event we have failed to foresee be catastrophic enough, it too will occur.

*

We should *want* to be crushed by the Inevitable, since, inevitably, we are.

*

Optimists hog so many illusions for themselves that there's none left for anybody else. Would they just learn to share, the whole world could live in a dream.

*

They are right, those who proclaim the end of the world has come. For some poor devil it always has.

*

A victim's heart is the best net ever invented for gathering knowledge.

*

Small as it is, the heart still manages to pack within itself more pain than there is salt in the ocean or truth in despair. No wonder it never stops bleeding!

*

No true passion perishes quietly.

*

To "destroy oneself" is to *assist* Fate.

*

We need to complain so much that, after exasperating the patience of men, we turn to prayer, and drive God up the wall as well.

*

Love is not blind. But at the edge of the abyss he covers his eyes before continuing forward.

*

"We are ill no longer now, but merely ruined." — It will be a red-letter day for the human race when at last it can legitimately avail itself of Tecmessa's consolation.

*

Time takes everything from us eventually, even our suffering. And of all her thefts, that is the one which our pride finds it hardest to forgive.

II.
Predicament and Impasse

After destroying ourselves and destroying God within ourselves, what is there left for us to do? — Admire the miraculous complacency of all those who have done neither.

*

We ought to delight more in seeing our dreams destroyed than in seeing them fulfilled. For fulfillment merely compromises what is best about them: their impossibility.

*

Were each of our triumphs not counterbalanced by a proportionate failure, their combined effect would probably be fatal. Fortunately, Providence has seen to this problem; and, by building into each piece of good fortune a suitable number of hazards and drawbacks, the guiding spirit of the cosmos has safeguarded our health. No sooner do we savor the bliss of a desire obtained than a corresponding loss or calamity drives us straight into the ground. And within this constant correction by disappointment lies the secret of our equilibrium — and, ultimately, our *salvation*.

*

Life is the most deliciously stupid of all disasters.

*

Whether disabused or ambitious, skeptical or fanatical, each of us feels some crazy need to finish what he's started. — Behold the hopeless loser hotfooting it to his doom, as if destroying himself constituted some kind of pressing obligation!

*

Supposing there are any rules for this game God is playing with us, they would appear to have quite conveniently slipped His mind.

*

To fall as magnificently as Lucifer fell, one must first have attained the heights Lucifer attained. I attained not even my natural height, but fell nevertheless — from my knees onto my face.

*

Liberated from our desires, we're dead; still subject to but one, we're enslaved.

*

Were there only some way to wash off that stain on our nothingness, the self!

*

The purest way of passing is to pass unnoticed.

*

Confusion, consciously sustained, is still the most effective defense there is against the solutions philosophy bombards us with.

*

The mind must be marvelously enamored of itself before Reason can build its nest there.

*

It is indeed Reason that governs the world: Reason *gone mad*.

*

How sweet to see Justice triumph! . . . So long as she's not triumphing over us.

*

Here in this universe where time and space themselves have teamed up to prevent us from satisfying all our desires — where they appear at every turn to hinder, limit, and taunt — man, in what we must suppose a most ironic frame of mind, has decided to set forth, in addition, thousands of laws.

*

Why does our detractor's face so often resemble our supporter's back? I await the coming of the anatomist who can explain.

*

Amateur of the interval, vampire of possibility, I have all my life see-sawed between balance and bitterness without ever managing to attain mastery in either realm. One moment I approach the consummate tranquility of the sage, and the next, the frenzied rage of the serial killer — but always I fall short of both baraka and bloodshed.

*

To understand nothing matters is to have understood too much.

*

Can error and confusion be transformed into positive values? *They must be* — unless we are bent on obliterating every last trace of the mind's prestige.

*

Every solution ushers in a new problem, more complicated than the one before. Better then to remain face-to-face with the original problem, refusing to budge.

*

At birth an impassable wall was thrown up before me against which I've been ambitiously banging my head for twenty-eight years.

*

Impossible to conjure up a more repellent image than that of a general *at prayer*.

*

God created woman because it was not good for man to be alone, and from that moment on man has been more alone.

*

Fiasco: a sure-fire method of redeeming yourself for having been so foolish as to act in the first place.

*

Of all the machines that have gone out of order, man alone enjoys the privilege of being *beyond repair*.

*

I am so estranged from Nature and from what is natural in myself that I react to my own instincts like someone who has seen a ghost.

*

There is but one reward for having surpassed all of your peers in some magnificent undertaking — a constant awareness of the utter futility of having done so.

*

No opportunity tempts true shyness. The timid man occupies a point even farther from this world than he who consciously shuns it.

*

Timidity and refinement are inefficacious weapons, it is true, weapons that wound those who wield them rather than their opponents. But they are weapons nevertheless. And the one poses as great a threat to the world's brutality as the other does to its vulgarity. Faced with the timid and the refined, the confident and the coarse do not feel themselves grow more powerful but more vulnerable. And if the former are wont to become the victims of the latter, it is not, as is sometimes believed, because they appear defenseless, but, on the contrary, because they *inspire fear*.

*

I still haven't managed to get over this embarrassment of mine about being human. Each time I remember what species I belong to, I blush.

*

What I most want is to be everyone, even those I shudder to think of. Oh, especially them!

*

It's hard to think of anything that would degrade God more than existence. Happy for Him that, unlike ourselves, He escaped such a humiliation!

*

"I think, therefore I am." Reply thus to anyone who holds that the consequences of thinking are anything but frightful and you shall have refuted him.

*

You can't be a success without compromising yourself. Indeed, simply by succeeding you do so.

*

If we are truly free of a failing, we don't pride ourselves on being so.

*

The dishonest man invokes principles where the honest one concedes a disposition.

*

Many an idea secretly entertains the ambition of toppling an empire.

*

Even the greatest dolt has cunning enough to hallucinate a world in which everyone but himself is to blame, and prudence enough to pass his days there, after bidding goodbye to the real one.

*

The stranger is not the man from another place but the man who is out of place wherever he is.

*

There is no way to make sense of the stupidity of this world. But then, why must we make sense of it? Perhaps reasoning is unnecessary, when one is capable of vomiting.

*

Writers are usually at their best when discoursing on subjects they know little or nothing about, for then they try all the harder to dazzle so as to disguise their ignorance.

*

To take control of the incoherent and create from it a second universe accessible to himself alone was once the unique privilege of the madman. But recently this privilege has been usurped by his imitator, the poet, and his admirer, the philosopher. Inferior types, no doubt — but men who at least have sufficient discernment to adopt the right model.

*

History is a catastrophe *in progress*.

*

Not until after we have lost all interest in a thing is its true value revealed to us.

*

Man is under God in much the same way as nothing is under Nothing.

*

A healthy man hoping to write a masterpiece is like a paralytic preparing to run a marathon.

*

None but the artist who creates unseen, in an atmosphere of complete indifference to his work, *really* creates. — When God created the universe the only praise He got is the praise He gave Himself (unstintingly enough, it's true).

*

There is no world deserving of annihilation but this one — a dubious honor, to be sure.

*

Woman was created *after* man. Just when one thought God couldn't come up with anything worse!

*

"For he who sees everything is from God, everything is the same" (Rumi). — Granted. But then, is not everything the same whether it's from God or not?

*

What else has man aspired to since Cain — or rather, since Adam — but to be accursed?

*

We hate our enemies less for the harm they do us than for the harm we do ourselves *through* them.

*

Wit is only tolerable when it's natural. The man who *wants* to be witty ceaselessly pursues you with his humor — an aggressive, tyrannical humor which, indisposed to withdraw and unable to relax, tries to force entry at every point of the conversation. Never-tiring, his jokes and quips follow you like the Furies, and you come to dread them as much.

*

Reading a great poet in translation is like drinking Chardonnay from a trough.

*

Is it plagiarism if we fail to give credit when quoting our double?

*

Now that man has succeeded in reducing God to nothing, I have decided to concern myself with nothing but God.

*

In my more tender moods I prefer not to think about how entirely unromantic must have been the God who created this universe in which it is possible to receive a paper-cut even when opening a love-letter.

*

"Be yourself." So has the monomaniac been advising the chameleon from time immemorial.

*

I acknowledge the existence of no one but God, with Whom I have a strict policy of no compromise.

*

Animals mind their own business unless they're attacked. Men attack because they're unable to mind their own business.

*

The barbarian was, for the ancient Roman, a threat; for the modern European, he's an ancestor.

*

A perfectly tolerant man would be totally without interest.

*

Whatever you do, don't fall into the trap of defending yourself. Next thing you know, you'll be defending a *cause!*

*

Everybody proceeds as if under a spell. Which is why, to fathom a person in his "deepest being," you need only grasp the particular way in which he's bewitched.

*

The professional — a thaumaturge who transforms persons into appointments.

*

The most amazing thing about the mediocre man is that, despite his total lack of accomplishment on every level, he remains a complete enigma.

*

Our desires are something we help create, not something we succumb to.

*

I pity the man consumed by rage in this world where nothing is *worth* destroying.

*

The creation of the Devil would seem to have been God's revenge on Himself, and seldom has vengeance been so well deserved.

*

By frankly proclaiming our faults we please our friends, but not our enemies; on the contrary, these latter resent us all the more for having *beat them to it.*

*

We are understandably reluctant to endorse the idea that everyone gets what he deserves. For while it satisfactorily accounts for the misfortunes of others, it fails to explain our own.

*

He admires pride most who has swallowed his for years.

*

So similarly sinister in their ways are the two sexes that were it not for a few anatomical practical jokes on the part of Nature, it would be almost impossible to tell them apart.

*

All beings deserve to be loved for something other than what, unfortunately, they *are.*

*

Philosophy reveals the inanity of reality, and reality, the inanity of philosophy.

*

I once believed there was no perfecter skeptic than myself. But I must have been fooled into finding more truth and purpose than I realized in these opinions and pursuits of mine from which I supposed myself so detached. How else to explain the fact that with each passing day I find even *less?*

*

The religious man is so made that he cannot for long devote himself to anything but the Nonexistent. He may flirt for a spell with objects real and graspable, but only to return with redoubled force to the realm of nameless enigmas. He would rather be given a promise than a prize, and would rather compose hymns to a phantom than sonnets to a woman. Whence the ridiculous success of God throughout the ages.

*

Chasing after dreams is a childish pursuit, and consequently best left to the poets and entrepreneurs of this world — to impassioned artists and cunning business men as they compete for prominence in their respective fields. It behooves the mature individual to remain on the sidelines, soberly documenting his gradual decay.

*

Sixty seconds ago I was totally enraged; now I'm perfectly calm. How little have I in common with that man of a minute before!

*

"So what happened?" — "The unthinkable, as usual."

*

Should the man who has everything lose but one thing, he feels as if all were lost.

*

Life joins us to what we abhor and reject with the same diabolical celerity as it divorces us from what we adore and depend on. The unforeseen disaster is Fate's masterstroke.

*

I have a knack for recognizing greatness when I see it. Particularly in God's mistakes.

*

Whatever affords us hope we must cast aside, and move forward from there — *if we can*.

*

Female beauty is the quicksand of the sensualist.

*

Unless you've felt the desire to throw yourself from a bridge during a fit of laughter, you haven't lived.

*

The nothingness of this universe so far outweighs our own that we cannot but feel impotent before it — impotent in the face of such *infinite* nullity.

*

All that needs to be expressed may be expressed in one sentence — what am I saying? in one *expletive!*

III.
A Few Twirls Around the Tomb

Death is no doubt Nature's best idea of all. But she hit upon it a little late — after having already unleashed life upon the world. It is with death that Nature ought to have *begun*.

*

Every hour an untold number of potential deviants and lunatics exits the womb and enters the world. They are removed from that oven of evil and brought into this kitchen of crime. As to how many cradles are the current whereabouts of future malefactors: I don't even want to think about it. They're multiplying at a truly alarming rate. Yet what sweetness and innocence emanate from the faces of these enemies of humanity at a mere six months! Who would guess that that baby whose cheek we pinch today might go on to butcher half a town in twenty-five years?

*

Those peoples of the past who responded to each new birth by weeping understood the proper use of tears. We moderns waste so many of ours on movies and popular songs that we've none left for *life*.

*

From Womb to Tomb is but a three-letter trip.

*

Childhood is a getting off on the wrong foot of which adulthood is the fatal misdevelopment.

*

One becomes human by dint of contemplating death without pause, by dint of dispensing with every other pursuit and occupation in order to commune with one's future corpse. So long as we fail to perceive that fatal point at which our blood stops flowing and to fasten our mind thereupon, we partake of quadrupedal nescience. Of course, not everyone is prepared to accept the Homo Sapiens challenge. Quite a few prefer the more comfortable course of affixing to their frame a couple of extra limbs wherewith to stealthily creep past the rigors of sustained thanatopsis. Indeed, this world abounds in nonagenarians with so little awareness of what mortality means that they might just as well have never been born!

*

My vision of the universe is so clear that if one day I were to awake to find everyone I had ever loved lying disemboweled in a heap before my bed, I would scarcely bat an eyelash.

*

Babies beautify death, because it exists in them in its *purest form*. In the adult death is totally corrupted.

*

Only what has fled from our minds never to return can we congratulate ourselves upon having conquered once and for all. Senility, too, is a kind of victory — perhaps the greatest one.

*

I go along with Life's plan in much the same way as someone who knows better might go along with a complete lunatic's.

*

A weak memory is one way of letting oneself off the hook.

*

There are bodies without a sexual destiny — bodies by which Nature is baffled, and which Desire assaults in vain.

*

If the unexpected appearance of a hearse can make our hair stand on end, how much more so the unexpected appearance of a baby-carriage — that *hearse for the newborn* . . .

*

I am on occasion subject to paroxysms of religiosity during which I would kill everyone in the world if I could, in order to be completely alone with God.

*

Incredible how much pain and misfortune we are prepared to put up with day after day, simply in order to die!

*

Any problem that might eventually push one to suicide is a problem with *potential*.

*

A charitable child always manages to forgive his mother for having failed to abort.

*

A rat embarks on the rather indelicate operation of cannibalizing one of his brothers by breaking open his skull and eating out his brains. And thereby this rodent pays a far higher tribute to the seat of the intelligence than the majority of men ever do.

*

He who has not spent his whole life in pain is so corpselike already that Death, when at last she arrives, hasn't the vaguest idea what to do with him. Finding here nothing spiritual, emotional, or intellectual that has ever really pulsed with life and hence might be decomposed, she quite naturally concentrates on the physical — and goes overboard.

*

Life is a question of intensity, not of time. A tortured poet lives more in twenty seconds than the rest of us do in twenty years.

*

Memory, that tête-à-tête with the Intolerable.

*

The problem with senility is that it always comes *too late*. A little softness of the brain would temper the trials of youth, and make middle age a more palatable experience.

*

He whose twin dies in the womb gets an unfair head-start on abandonment. How are the rest of us, forlorn as we may be, to compete with a person who was *born* feeling left behind?

*

Once again I have decided to go on living. That is to say, I shall enter into further negotiations with Vulgarity.

*

A great source of relief when we are young, the idea of suicide becomes increasingly problematic as the years pass, increasingly fraught with complication. Entertaining it is not so delectable at thirty-three as it was at sixteen, because each time we experience afresh the desire to kill ourselves we must face the fact that we lacked the good sense to do so long ago. And thus what began as a tonic is transformed into yet another reason for self-reproach.

*

There are some things it is better not to do, and being born is one of them.

*

Whoever hasn't lived at least half his life in a fever hasn't lived at all.

*

Debauchery is what Virginity becomes upon acquiring a work ethic.

*

The memory of the pain *completes* the pain. A wound is not truly a wound until remembered.

*

The mere idea of Eternal Life leaves me gasping for air. To *survive* an ordeal of that magnitude, you would have to be either a complete idiot or a complete monster — or, as in the case of God, a perfectly balanced combination of both.

*

You cannot *think yourself to death*, because death is where thought *begins*, the capacity for intellectual advancement presupposing as it does a radical disunion with life.

*

At peace with themselves and the world, even the most brilliant men appear intellectually comatose. It takes the prospect of a massacre to awaken the mind.

*

Every day I feel compelled to punish myself for still being alive — as if still being alive weren't already punishment enough!

*

There is no *enlightened* desire. The desire to die nearly qualifies as such, but not quite.

*

Just what Nature is after I don't know, unless it should be a slow and painful death at the hands of her favorite species.

*

Supposing this life to be some kind of undisclosed intelligence test, I doubt any but suicides are getting passing grades.

*

Celibacy is a sort of sneering of the genitals at Nature.

*

The perpetually recurring memory of our most painful experiences is our punishment for having survived them.

*

There are men to whom life can offer nothing, because everything life has to offer is nothing to them. They are like plants whose roots have never tasted water and whose leaves have never been touched by the sun, and yet which, by some sinister miracle, *live* — in much the same way as a skeleton might live, were a skeleton alive.

*

Had only she miscarried, the Virgin Mary could have saved the world.

*

Despite his less formidable physical design, man, like every beast of prey, is a *born killer*. What he lacks in fangs and claws he more than makes up for in malice and ammunition.

*

When a man leaps to his death from a rooftop, where does he land? — On the sidewalk below, from our point of view. But from his point of view, who knows? perhaps right in the middle of the second movement of Bach's harpsichord concerto in E major!

*

Were all women now pregnant cast forward in time but a few decades, they would be carrying coffins in their bellies, not embryos, and in concert they could give birth to — a graveyard.

*

The only blow that deserves to be called mortal is the one dealt at birth.

*

I am so completely permeated by the poison of life that even were I to die a hundred million deaths I still wouldn't be dead enough to experience the relief *one* death affords others.

*

Sure method of putting yourself in an excellent mood — journey back in your imagination to approximately nine months before the moment of your birth and *stop time* . . .

*

For the prematurely dead removal to a tomb is but a minor inconvenience.

*

Whatever falls outside of death's domain partakes of madness. Most notably, life itself . . .

*

So many men I admire have killed themselves during a stay in Paris that it's really something of a miracle I'm not more inclined to doubt the merit of anyone who visits that city and *lives*.

*

If all murders ever pondered could be simultaneously accomplished, nobody would be left standing. Close the gap between imagination and action and you turn the world into a vulture's paradise.

*

The single best therapy for all of life's catastrophes is *forgetting how to breathe* . . .

*

Suicide is purely a matter of convenience. When in the grip of rage or despair we want to kill someone. And, as it happens, the first person we encounter is — ourself.

*

Sexual intercourse is hardly an adequate substitute for the profound connection which violently killing each other affords. But in societies where intimacy is banned, the bed must do overtime to make up for the blade's prohibition.

*

Anyone who is capable of absorbing the essential truths at all will have done so by, let's say,

. . . seventeen; after which nothing remains for him to do but *die of them.*

*

Death is a definitive break with all of life's nonsense — a wild plunge into meaning from which we never emerge.

*

I am a little too melancholy to be a killer, to *realize* my rage, which is counterbalanced by a tendency to mope . . . Were there but one less drop of sadness in my blood, I would have slaughtered everyone around me before turning eighteen.

*

Nobody is ever *without* his death, but many a man carries it around with him all his days as if he were a courier, and it a sealed document addressed to somebody else.

*

I'm not sure the cunning, the shrewd, or even the merely practical are so secure in this world as they think, and when I imagine their possible fate I long to protect them. For at any moment divine caprice or occult vicissitude may turn all the timid dreamers out there into mass-murderers. And when that happens, any head not buried in the clouds will be at risk of being cut off.

*

That old torturer, Eternity, vouchsafes Death the body, on condition that the soul be brought back to her *alive*.

*

The man who lives as if he might not die at any moment displays an astounding lack of foresight.

*

Were I a worm, there are corpses I simply couldn't bring myself to feed upon. I would dine in a way my peers would no doubt deem *fastidious*.

*

At a certain point to go on living becomes absurd — at the moment of our birth, in fact.

*

The cosmically-minded man dreams of a suicide in harmony with the whole of nature. Simply leaping from a cliff isn't good enough for him. He insists on leaping from a cliff at twilight's end and disappearing from sight at the same moment as the sun.

*

When we consider the probable consequences of acting, as compared with those of abstaining, we are likely to conclude, along with Hamlet, that procrastination is the way to go. Except, of course, where suicide is concerned. What a heavy price we pay each time we postpone our own personal adventure in cyanide!

*

Don Juan is what Werther turns into when his suicide attempt fails.

*

Necromaniacal goal of today's mystic: to die into a God *Himself* dead.

*

From the end of the world there perpetually emanates a gaiety never surpassed.

*

If we are to succeed at suicide, we must first have the discipline to pare down our enthusiasm for death to a single method. The man of luxuriant leanings who demands too rich a variety from his final moment is unlikely to attain that liberation from consciousness he has so long dreamt of. Behold him there, compassionate reader, torn between gas and poison, rope and razorblade, cliff and oncoming train: paralyzed by the complete impossibility of killing himself *in every possible way!*

*

If sexual desire rose up from the loins even half so discreetly as the howls of the damned do from Hell, inhabiting a body might be almost as tolerable as eternal damnation.

*

Man's fear of death is a well-documented fact, but when the time comes we all get up the courage to die — including those of us who hadn't enough to live.

*

"At this moment my life has officially come to an end!" — A pronouncement I've made on so many different occasions that I'm no longer sure just how I should *date* my cadaver.

*

The question most deserving of attention today is not: "What is death?" but rather: "What is life?" For *our way of life* is already an answer to the first question.

*

Laughter seems to me the most important experience a man can have: the only one in life (aside from death) that *matters*.

*

This world's collapse would provide the ideal soundtrack for an astral dream. Happy the man who, come the Apocalypse, finds himself fast asleep on a distant star.

*

It is much to the honor of the birds and the beasts that they accept the corpse as a *limit*, and do not look for ways to linger beyond death. Unfortunately, the same cannot be said of man, whose notorious want of discretion in this matter has always been a source of fear, coloring everything from our burial practices to our funeral customs. Can one imagine a moth or a porpoise being so unmannerly as to return as a troubled spirit to terrorize the living? Man alone of all the creatures refuses to disappear politely at his appointed hour. He alone lays plans for leaving behind in this world a lasting and none too pleasant reminder of himself, in much the same manner as the slug leaves behind a trail of slime.

*

Fits of crying don't actually kill us, they just leave us *feeling* dead. And for this a deficiency in our anatomy is to blame. Two eyes simply aren't enough to accommodate a being built to cry around the clock. Such a being should be *all eyes,* in the same way that a fish is all scales or a porcupine all quills. In a moment of sorrow, Cassandra asks for ten thousand eyes — not enough to satisfy my greed, I fear, but still, a nice start. Every human being should be covered with eyes from head to foot. When we want to die, it is humiliating to have to depend on the sea's help: we should be able to drown in our own tears.

*

The illusion laughed at the cat: you have only nine lives?

Book the Second

Diabolical Fidelity

Why should the Devil work so hard to overthrow mankind when we are perfectly capable of overthrowing ourselves? Not just *capable*. We are veritable *virtuosos* of self-destruction, the number of techniques we have devised to that end being nothing short of mind-boggling. Creatures from less imaginative kingdoms can only gape in wonder as they watch us ring the changes on madness and multiply the faces of dolor. Yet despite endless proof of our zeal for the flames, Lucifer can't relax. In fact the faster we drop, the more jittery Eve's famous seducer and Jesus's famous tempter becomes, repeatedly prompted to further nefarious enterprise by the nagging fear that he might just be expendable after all. And so it is that rather than rejoicing over our voluntary compliance with his plans, this perfectionist sulks, and broods, and kicks himself day and night for not pushing us all the more quickly into that gulf at once sulfurous and caliginous where, with the downward velocity of a diving plane, we are already headed. Has never-ending torment taught him no patience?

I suspect that all of this running to and fro without a moment's rest is beginning to tell on his health. Just think how long it's been since the King of Craft launched his sublunar career with that celebrated incident in the garden! A perfectly orchestrated prank. A masterpiece of tact and subtlety. He could — and should — have retired on that note, an acknowledged master of seduction. But no. Since then his fascination with God's favorite fool has grown apace. According to one conservative estimate it has quadrupled weekly since the Deluge. So what wonder if nowadays each revolution of the second-hand should afford us a fresh example of his handiwork? Hell must be going to rack and ruin with all the time he who is supposed to be in charge there puts in here! Or could it be that, weary and overworked as he is, Satan has lost all sense of his whereabouts and can no longer distinguish terrestrial from infernal, man from friend, city from circle of Hell? An understandable mistake. On more than one occasion I have confused them myself.

But this is an angel popularly reputed second only to God in knowledge and power, and in the view of some clearer-sighted (and hence less heeded) theologians, above Him in both. And while I can imagine a being so esteemed confusing Our World with the Underworld, I can't imagine him making the much bigger mistake of deeming his presence in the garden indispensable. Are we to believe he didn't know that long before he slithered up, or flew in, or whatever a snake with wings does (perhaps a bit of both) — are we to believe he didn't know that those specialists in perdition, Adam and Eve, had planned out their fall down to the last detail, and so had no need of his assistance? Clearly the Creator had every confidence in their ability to self-destruct alone and unaided. Let us not depict Him as some sort of Celestial Set-Up Artist prompted by mischievous caprice to place the accursed tree in the center of the garden. In fact He merely wanted to ensure that the fruit could be conveniently gotten at. Since the eating was inevitable, why not make the locating quick? Determined to spare Eve the anxiety of combing Eden in vain quest of her favorite plant, God was good enough to put it right in front of her nose. So then, Satan: what need was there for you to wing your way into Paradise to persuade her to eat thereof? And did you really need to go so far as to *disguise yourself?* Don't get me wrong, the reptilian get-up was great — fabulous, in fact; but I'm not sure I see the point in it, any more than I see the point in precipitating by a few days a foredoomed event.

Frankly, I can't figure out why someone with so much cosmic clout would feel any desire to be associated with some second-rate delinquent made of dirt. Is it man's criminal inclinations you find alluring? His crimes are undeniably numerous and ambitious, but I trust you perceive them to be as devoid of TRUE REALITY as his acts of benevolence. Man espouses and produces nothing but simulacra. Do you suppose that you can lift him up to the level of Evil, as God had once hoped to lift him up to the level of Good? Well, I hate to be the bearer of bad tidings, but since man makes his home on a plane infinitely beneath Good and Evil, he hasn't the slightest hope of ever reaching them, let alone of going *beyond* them, as a certain leg-puller once proposed. You're kidding yourself, Satan, if you think this mud-clod has a future! Why not depart forthwith from this fool planet where the foolishest of all creatures builds, bustles, and pontificates with an air of fantastic importance? The only thing earth and its feckless lord and conqueror could possibly afford you is material for jokes. So maybe you should just forget about trying to make man meet demonic standards and bend your energies toward the achievement of some more compassable goal, like organizing a *Comedy Hour* in Hell. Let the damned laugh a little as they burn; and don't be afraid to laugh a little yourself. So ridiculously serious is man, and so seriously does he take himself and his opinions and his occupations, that it behooves the whole rest of the universe to burst into long peals of laughter to compensate. Laugh at earth and its notorious hijacker, Lucifer — and let all of Hell laugh with you! And now that you're learning to let go some and to take things a little more lightly than you did before I became your counselor, I just have to ask: Are you aware that your abhorred enemy in Heaven was sensible enough to abandon long ago this realm you still haunt? Yes, you heard me right. Fearing His alliance with man was bringing Him bad luck, God broke all ties with this blasted jinx — and I can't say I blame him. He even went so far as to blot the Milky Way from the Empyrean maps, as a precautionary measure. For Him this whole galaxy is as good as gone, and may as well never have existed. Not only does He no longer answer the prayers which we, in our impertinence, continue to pelt Him with, but He won't even stoop to the more entertaining tasks of commanding fathers to sacrifice their sons, turning women into pillars of salt, and devising floods of a breadth and force to cover the face of the world. There are so many cities that deserve to go down in flames (all of them, in fact) but no Gabriel is being sent to take care of the job, as in the good old days of Sodom and Gomorrah. You alone, with an obduracy bordering on blindness, persist in mixing with men and in finding some kind of merit in their deluded undertakings. To what is your fidelity to be attributed, infernal prince, frivolity or lack of taste?

The Genealogy of Denial

If denial comes more naturally to us, and fits us more comfortably, than knowledge, it is doubtless because the very universe we inhabit *springs* from denial. Upon pulling each new addition to the Creation out of His hat, God called it Good. No opinions were solicited, no tests conducted, no results observed. The wheels of the newly assembled cosmic machine hadn't even turned once, and there was God playing the fiddle of His Own impeccable craftsmanship. As He haughtily informs a less than enthusiastic Lucifer in *The Tragedy of Man:* Homage Only, Not Censure Is My Due. With an attitude like that is it any wonder He could only put up with our first parents so long as they lived in complete ignorance of their Creator's nature, their own nature, and the nature of the cosmos? The prospect of another Lucifer with eyes that see and ears that hear was understandably repugnant to a Creator so manifestly flawed. Bent as He was on keeping the truth about Himself at bay, what He needed were not scientists of His weaknesses but dumb affirmations of His divinity: a couple of puppets in Paradise devoted to singing His praises day and night. And so as soon as He found out about the whole apple business, He pounced on Adam and Eve in a panic and proceeded to beat all of the bright ideas out of them — needlessly, as it turns out. They were already disenchanted enough by what they had seen and needed no further encouragement to once again close their eyes. Having peered a little too deeply into the universe and into themselves, they concluded that clairvoyance wasn't all it was cracked up to be. And ever since that day Denial has been the rule, on earth as it is in Heaven.

The Worst Wait

Of all the languages, Spanish alone is sufficiently fearless to fathom the essence of what we call *Hope*. This particular word of ours, with all its warm and comforting connotations, is one hundred percent humbug. And there is something even more soft and alluring (and hence, even more misleading) about its French equivalent: *Espoir*. The French have not scrupled to denote one of the direst plagues of the human mind by one of the loveliest-sounding words in their language, thereby brilliantly distinguishing themselves in the sphere of euphonic sophistry. But beneath the fair music of those two syllables lies the abyss. Or was Buddha, are we to suppose, of so sportive a bent as to have put a ban on Hope for nothing? Even Quintilian, no seeker after truth but a mere teacher of rhetoric, belonging to a race of road-builders too dim-witted to dream of anything but universal empire, felt compelled to include *Spes* on his list of evil passions. But instead of heeding these men's clairvoyant advice and keeping clear of this hydra, we have taken it for a house-pet. We have rashly ventured to *domesticate* Hope. More level-headed and less in love with total let-downs, we should never have launched this questionable concept in the first place, let alone have allowed it to sail freely through our everyday discourse, flying the flag of its utter falseness. Nobler, honester, and in every sense prudenter, the Spaniard does not assign Hope its own separate, more privileged compartment in his language, but makes it share the floor with *wait*. *Espera* is the better part of *Esperanza* — and one and the same verb, *Esperar*, does the work for both. And this is as it should be. For, fundamentally, waiting is what hoping is — nothing more, nothing higher. Strip away all of the meretricious tinsel from Hope and what you're left with is a *wait*. And it may just be the worst wait you've ever had.

The Unenlightened

Reincarnation is pretty annoying, not to mention humiliating, but I think I've finally gotten used to it. I'm no longer going to let myself be seduced by Nirvana's charms. I'm done competing for the prize of permanent extinction. How could I ever have considered myself a candidate for transcendence? I don't even deserve to approach the void, let alone dissolve into it! My fate — which I now accept, uncomplaining — is to return continually to this crowd of dimwits who, like myself, have been "held back," who have gotten glued to the earth's surface on account of their failure to grasp Truth. The worst of our class, we've now seen not just the wise but even the merely competent brush past us into nonexistence, as we hold fast to flesh and bones, nursing the same old desires and entertaining the same old delusions as if they were absolutely new — as if we hadn't already nursed and entertained them a million times before. The human face is all too familiar to us, we who have not yet rid ourselves of it. And I admit that my embarrassment at still wearing one here in the Kali Yuga, at the tail end of an entire cycle, is so immense that I've sometimes looked for someone to blame, sought out a scapegoat for my carnal persistence. But who am I kidding? Haven't I had plenty of opportunities to earn my death through detachment? And I let them slip every time! That's why I've decided to admit I'm no good at playing the spiritual game. I belong among all these bad students who make up the world's population today, these blockheads barred from enlightenment, lacking the pizzazz to catapult themselves beyond the realm of Maya. But seeing as we're stuck here, why should we have to keep going through the tedious routine of changing bodies and identities every few decades? If nothing else, we should be allowed to wear the same suit of skin for eighty thousand years, like Vipassi back in the good old days. This continual womb-hopping is a real hassle, and it isn't exactly conducive to forming lasting attachments. Considering how frequently we switch them, it's practically a miracle we manage to distinguish the women who bear us from shuttle-buses!

Laughter and Logic

Even the most malign laughter is not without innocence; whereas logic, when it is malign, is *totally* malign. Which isn't to say that it wouldn't be a little foolish to invite to a hospital or a funeral a man who derives hilarity from others' misfortunes. But otherwise he's harmless enough. Far more to be feared are those who seek to justify any form of suffering by dint of rational argument. Those who, desperate to confer legitimacy on the manifold evils of life, press into service metaphysical concepts like Karma and Providence. Yet it is the laughers, not the philosophers, who give us the creeps. And that is because laughter, unlike discourse, does not admit of question or contradiction. Laughter is *absolute*. And there is something else about these hyenas of mishap nobody likes: they aren't afraid to *enjoy themselves*.

The Infernal Lure

No howl, supplication, or teardrop lacks the power to impede our Pilgrim on his journey to Paradise. He is a wine-taster of woe, a tourist of torment, crawling through those dolorous circles at a snail's pace, as if he feared nothing so much as a moment's relief. What'll it be then: fierce punishments presented seriatim or beholding at last the blessed countenance of your beloved Beatrice? Dante shouts for the first, and shows he means it by refusing to abandon his slow-poke ways and blast rocket-like into Heaven. Hey, if you're more at home among sighs and cries than angelic songs, why not drag your feet? Catching sight of yet another victim of the divine plan, he stops in his tracks and gets ready to gulp down yet another devastating tale. He's got a real hankering to hear horrors recounted — to amass them in his mind — to collect, label, and arrange what revolts the heart. And so when he finally manages to wrench himself away from all of that punishment and repentance and finds himself in the Empyreal Regions, standing before that beautiful and radiant damsel who is the supposed goal of his great trudge, he can muster up no more than a few joyous exclamations which, I'm sorry to say, ring absolutely false. Can it be that Hell has rubbed off on him, altering his most fundamental feelings and desires? Is it possible that in the fiery pit he found delights which dwarf those of love? One thing's for sure: to return now to any kind of Cavalcantian nonsense is out of the question. The face of a lover no longer suits him. And nor does the voice. It is really quite painful to hear the words he addresses to the girl of his dreams (Virgil respectfully holds his tongue, but is hardly taken in). Only his interviews with the damned carry conviction. He ought to have extended his stay in the lower depths, lingered there awhile: why not? it would only have cost literature two rather superfluous levels of the afterworld.

The Devil's story is a different one. And how differently he went about things when pursuing the reverse adventure! Loath to tarry in Paradise plucking harps and intoning Hosannas, he plunged like a lightning-bolt into eternal blackness. Abyssward he sped without brakes, zipping right through every red light on the cosmic highway, as full of impatience to soak luxuriously in his first flame-bath as the myriad lost legions that followed in his wake. So delicious is Hell that I have no doubt Dante would have hung it around his neck and taken it up to Paradise with him, had that only been possible. And nor would anyone in his place have done otherwise — man, angel, or God. This Last, let us remember, placed Hell parallel to Heaven at a direct vertical drop so that He could spend all eternity gazing down into its howling depths, voyeuristically participating in the tortures continually being devised and perpetrated there. The appetite of everything in this universe, from the tiniest bug to the Supreme Being, points to torment as steadily and infallibly as the needle of a compass to the North. And that is why, like Lucifer, men are cast unprotestingly from beatitude into torment; but when it comes to parting ways with torment and taking a bite of beatitude — or even the merest *taste* — we hesitate, like our Pilgrim, unpropelled. Employing every means at our disposal, we multiply the obstacles between ourselves and bliss. And, accommodating as it is, Christian Eschatology has decided to assist us in this enterprise. It has in fact taken the trouble to set up an entire *penal system* there. And for this we are profoundly indebted to it. Any religion that makes salvation into an almost impossible privilege, granted to fewer men each five thousand years than you can count on your fingers and toes, while pushing the rest of us down into the flames we prefer with all of the weight of Divine Justice, does us a service we can never repay.

Stoicism's Mistake

If Stoicism never really "hit the big time," if compared to Christianity, its competitor back in the days of the deliquescent empire with whom it struggled to gain possession of the Western mind, it must be regarded as a complete failure, it is because Stoicism did not see how satisfying it is to refine and diversify torments. It did nothing to encourage or validate man's tendency to cultivate the Intolerable. On the contrary, the Stoics proposed ways for rising above pain — drew up a whole program whose sole purpose was to help us rid ourselves of what we cherish most. How could such perversity succeed? Aware that man does not desire to escape pain but to stuff himself full of it, the Christians took a more sensible approach. They spared no expense in concocting prickly situations, rolling out punishments, projecting ominous signs of impending doom everywhere. There was no idea so debilitating that these promoters of the apocalypse, addicts of insomnia, persecutors and defiers of the flesh shrunk from promulgating it as absolute truth. Going to any lengths to gratify our weakness for the Worst, they made masochism into a virtue and martyrdom into a goal. And for the grand finale, they decided to represent their *god* as crucified: a brilliant marketing strategy which by itself would have ensured this religion's unprecedented success and persistent sway throughout the ages. How could any pagan philosophy hope to compete with a spectacle like that?

Where God and Man Meet

A god that gets up the crazy idea of visiting earth disguised as a Palestinian Jew during the reign of Tiberius in hopes of causing an extraordinary ruckus, incurring accusation, and eclipsing all His creatures in victimhood is not a god any *normal* man is going to want to be associated with, let alone worship. But, luckily for divine vanity, human beings are anything but normal. We are, in fact, Nature's *freaks*. And that is why, far from blushing with embarrassment or recoiling in complete disgust from our Creator's masochistic exploits, we secretly relish them, kneeling down before His crucified image with an understanding wink.

Termite as Exemplar

To what lengths won't we go to escape the curse of consciousness? When we see ourselves playing at careers, inebriating ourselves with obligations, carefully elaborating and then dutifully fulfilling every form of foolish office — each decade we concoct hundreds of new tasks ranging from the totally needless to the absolutely senseless and allow ourselves to be consumed by them — we are forced to conclude that slavery is the human way of relaxing, freedom man's greatest fear, and that, so far as our species is concerned, bondage alone has the gift of conferring lightness. Our terror of the aimless unemployment of our simian ancestors — or rather, of the revelations about ourselves which we rightly suspect would result therefrom — has prompted us to ransack Nature in search of an alternative, and it is none other than the termite, that eminent precursor of the industrialist, whom our lust for constant activity has fixed upon to gratify itself. Some day, no doubt, we will be nearly indistinguishable from our chosen model, but at present there is no way we can conceal what clumsy and inefficient workers we are by comparison. Only in our very busiest moments do we seem to approach the level of this peerless insect — do we seem to acquire the termite's *wings*.

Ave Caesar!

Let us bid farewell to the Mind: it has no future. The barbarism which gave birth to the modern languages has declined into a *sub-barbarism* which is rapidly engulfing the entire globe. The ability to discern, distinguish, and profitably compare is vanishing; and soon the merest suggestion of an abstraction will evoke total bewilderment. Think of how many words of subtlety and complexity have already fallen into desuetude, and of how many more will soon follow. *Zeitgeist* lingers yet, but one wonders why, since in our time there is no *Geist*, only *Zeit* — no Spirit, only Time. Western man, in order to facilitate his pursuit of material wealth, has been forced to liquidate an entire spiritual heritage. But he has accomplished this with superb aplomb, and is now in the process of elaborating a means of expression in conformity with his particular deficit. From the rubble of contemporary languages a new language will emerge, one suited to the powers and purposes of this *new man* who is already today's *common man,* and who will be tomorrow's *only man* — a language as far inferior to our modern ones as these latter are to Latin and Greek. Present tendencies make it possible to predict the chief attributes of this sub-barbaric language of the future. The complete antithesis of Sanskrit, it will be completely *tangible.* It will cater to and encourage nothing but action, while obviating reflection of any sort. It will possess the same "spirit" as Caesar's vocabulary — i.e., no spirit at all. An empty language for a totally material animal. A language of objects, actions, and brute sensations, void of all sensibility, refinement, and nuance. If but one month belongs to Julius now — a month to which he has tenaciously clung for over two millennia — soon enough he will have taken the rest of the year captive. And not until then will Caesarian rule truly begin.

Social Convenience of the False Concept

The most shocking occurrences are not rare occurrences but rather common occurrences we are disinclined to acknowledge as such. Thus it is shocking to learn that a lady who has just sent us a polite note, has sent someone else we know a malicious letter. How can such a charming smile and such a terrifying scowl belong to one and the same face? We know that they do, because the victim of the letter has brought it to us, expressing a distress which, if somewhat exaggerated, is nevertheless genuine. And we know, furthermore, quite apart from any proofs offered by personal experience, and just as certainly as philosophers know what they term *a priori* truths, that society is absolutely infested with facsimiles of Iago. While smiling at us, a person may scowl at another, whether because he is dexterously turning his face back and forth between the two, or because, like Janus, he has two faces.

Still, we do not like to think that both pieces of writing could have been composed by one and the same person, since the portrait of the author which emerges from a comparison of the two is anything but pleasing. In the polite note, where is sincerity? Convention itself could have dictated every line. Whereas the nasty letter is alive from start to finish, and burns with the fire of true feeling. The first does as much to conceal, as the last to reveal, the personality behind the pen.

But since for society to exist at all, legerdemain must triumph over truth and convention gag emotion, we bring forth the note's false sentiments as evidence of "innate goodness" and depreciate the importance of the more troublesome epistle. To tell the truth, we altogether dismiss the epistle, on the grounds that it is but the inconsequential explosion of a "mood." And thus a none too reassuring revelation of questionableness of character is improved into the fruit of a mere fleeting spasm, and any meddlesome doubts we may have had are duly put to bed.

The Attractions of Rage

In my serener, more pacific moods I am tempted to abjure rage and devote myself completely to sadness — which is, without a doubt, the nobler, more refined emotion. But sadness has the serious drawback of being cosmically void. When sad, we shrink up into a little ball and become peripheral to being. Rage, on the other hand, permits (in fact, compels) us to expand beyond ourselves and become *vaster*. It launches us beyond the terrestrial into the sidereal, where, with the demonic glee of a mischievous child, we proceed to crush the stars one by one. You can paddle lethargically down a river of tears; or, unfettered and full of lethal zest, you can leap and swim through infinite space, blowing dust clouds all over the place, kicking planets off course, and stomping entire galaxies to powder. The centrifugal virtues of rage seduce to transcendence. Of all the emotions, none is more cosmic, not even Love, whose expansive potential is sadly crippled by its confined scope. Promising to carry us above common experience into a magical realm where we shall be lighter, freer, and without limitations, love ends by clipping the wings it lent and plunging us all the more deeply into the human morass; it cements us into that very species which, by grace of its glittering promise, we had hoped to escape. But the enraged man leaps over humanity to become a veritable Satanic force, vibrating expansively outward in waves of pure malevolence to the remotest boundaries of life and being. The universe is seized and consumed by his wrath. His furor, like some diabolical perfume, is ceaselessly diffused through the farthest reaches of space. And the cosmos, having no choice but to succumb, breaks to pieces like a blown egg in his fist.

River and Whirlpool

Were the average man's soul a sieve for all of the terrors of the cosmos, the linear conception of time could never have caught on. It is because his essence partakes of the plant's, because he is closer to the somnolence of chlorophyll than to the disquietude of consciousness that this notion of a forward-marching time has triumphed. Men wounded by consciousness could never have conceived of such a time and nor do they succeed in obtaining a foothold in it now, since for them time does not advance but *pulls down*. The ravaged-from-birth whirlpool their way through life; while the affectively vacant rush forward river-fashion, seizing all they can in passing and dragging it forward in the pitiless current of their complete nothingness.

Omnia Amor Vincit

Love is born when rape, encountering civilization, begins to reflect on itself. Being contrary to Nature's harsh imperatives, love requires a factitious setting in which to grow and flourish; and like all that is beautiful, gentle, and sweet, it rides on the back of instinctual decline. As man's will is corrupted and his cruelty succumbs to softer influences, so does the uncompromising demand degenerate into a cajoling sonnet, the lecherous grin into a shy smile, the firm grip into a gentle caress. At length virility gives way to debility, and the blood-stained alleyway of a besieged town is abandoned in favor of the comfort of a perfumed bedroom, where night after night Refinement inflicts a humiliating defeat on the instincts.

New Enemies

Our mechanical and technological enemies are multiplying so quickly that I am surprised anyone still bothers with human ones. I am not so brash as to deny that we human beings are loathsome monsters, and that all of our races, religions, and nations deserve to be annihilated on the spot (were it only possible, I would annihilate them all myself, beginning with my own). But how to take an interest in the human epidemic in this age of ingenious devices? I am so busy day and night battling machines and appliances that I hardly ever dream of massacres anymore. Which is quite remarkable, since in my youth I seldom dreamt of anything else. For awhile I was so filled with murderous rage that I regarded anyone in the same room with myself as a *potential corpse*. But screens, dials, and circuit boards have distracted me from my lofty goal of liquidating our entire species and led me into a labyrinth of trifles. Each new invention, I have discovered, provokes, aggravates, and maddens in its own particular way; and I plan, at some point, to enumerate and distinguish between these. As a result of progress, we now live entangled in so many petty problems and frustrations; but there is no lack of objects to lash out at for relief. Has not picking on others become passé? *obsolete*, even? Granted, in the old days it was impossible to get any pleasure out of life without persecuting or exterminating *someone;* but thanks to material advancement, we now enjoy the amazing convenience of being able to take on a new opponent each time we change rooms. There are computers to kick, food processors to fling, televisions to hurl obscenities at. How wonderful to be able to wage a full-scale war without ever leaving home! to no longer need to wade through rivers of blood on the way to our next victim! Of course, the connoisseur of carnage may regret this. But the fact is that the machine is an even more provoking beast than our neighbor; and never have man's cruel impulses been so pampered as now.

Suicide, Virginity, and Tears

If we reject uniquely human achievements like suicide, virginity, and tears in favor of pursuits in every sense ridiculous and vulgar — the sort of pursuits which only an unhinged ape or a hyena in his cups could be expected to applaud — it is not because we are ignorant of the glory they bring, but because we wish to be as considerate as possible of the feelings of inferior species. Why terrorize the birds of the air and the beasts of the field with continual proofs of an unapproachable loftiness? To flaunt just how much further we can go than they in sadness and solitude would be too cruel. For us, even the idea of "Evolution" was but a polite concession. We stopped bragging about being made in God's image the moment we saw the devastating effect it was having on the gorilla's self-esteem.

Rise of the Pharmaceutical

 The anti-depressant has supplanted Christianity as the most popular method of coping, as Christianity once supplanted philosophy; so that today's priest finds himself in the same position as Julian the Apostate: an obdurate champion of beliefs that have breathed their last. But the priest still inspires a certain amount of respect, even if merely pretended, unlike the sage. Things were not always thus. Time was when the bewildered man sought out a sage to show him that his pains were mere opinions; now he opens a bottle of pills and proceeds to read the newspaper. After being laid out flat on our backs by Fate, it is not the teachings of the wise we turn to but Psychiatry, Chemistry, and other proofs of Modern Progress. Enlightenment? Obsolete. Our confidence belongs exclusively to that new breed of man — the mirific emanation of this perfectest of all epochs — known as the Professional or the Expert. And woe to any Epicurus, Epictetus, or similar mountebank without a degree who dares enter our midst! Regarding all knowledge rooted in true understanding with merciless skepticism, we believe only in help that can be *bought*. Prostitution is our religion, and he who refuses to whore himself out the heretic we persecute. Shame on Socrates for having shirked his obligation to peddle the Dialectic! and how infamous of this self-styled "physician of the soul" who attended not a single day of medical school to have censured the Sophists for charging for their services! We are disposed to dispute the competence of anyone who *doesn't*. Further evidence of our acumen may be found in the fact that we have brought forth the first method of treating despair fully compatible with Commerce. As for those past cultures that looked upon mercantile pursuits as necessary but lowly, where the business man had his rightful place in the social scheme but was not permitted to wield power or determine life's tone — how appallingly backward! Haven't we exposed as pure naïveté the belief that there are nobler pursuits in life than making a profit? Even emotional trauma may be transformed into material opulence — and what blockheads all who came before us must have been to have let such an opportunity slide! Leave spirituality to monetary morons and outcasts of the Career — to men incapable of grasping the high mysteries of Economics. Were Seneca alive today he would have to concede that not only is our pharmaceutical approach more lucrative but it is also more *effective* than the outmoded spiritual approaches of the Porch and the Hammock. Doubtless the ancients would not have taken Stoicism and Epicurism so seriously had they only possessed the Periodic Table.

The Last Prophet

It was April of 1990 and I was standing in the Strasbourg station waiting for a train to Paris when there arose suddenly and seemingly from out of nowhere a haggard and hunchbacked old man in a condition of dress best described as wildly dilapidated, who began shouting the most frightful gibberish in my face. To this day I remain a little baffled as to why he chose *me* as the confidante of his rancor. Perhaps I looked sympathetic? or, likelier yet: *interested*. His ebullition was impressive — but not quite so impressive, to my mind, as the complete insouciance of everyone nearby. No doubt about it, I was in a city of somnambulists, the sole exception to which was this hallucinatory figure who had forced himself upon my solitude: this man of monstrous aspect from whom the whole world withdrew in horror — my new "friend."

On every side, zombies with their heads buried in newspapers: people so engrossed in *reading* about recent events that they were apparently incapable of appreciating — or even so much as noticing — one presently taking place. These victims of their own education and minions of the Roman Alphabet, having opted for literacy over actuality, no longer had any passage to the latter, it would appear. They had lost either the desire, or the ability, to experience life directly. For them an event could not be called significant, important, or even *real* unless it had taken the form of an *article*. Substance they vouchsafed not to the thing itself but to its printed reflection. Ghosts grabbing at shadows . . .

And yet here in their midst was, for all they knew, the last prophet, having emerged for a moment from the mute gulf of his fathomless despair to admonish mankind. Is it because I was the only one there not reading, the only one there who appeared prepared to experience pain and wretchedness *off the page*, that he singled me out for his sermon? There's no way to know. But feeling myself somehow honored by his attentions, I stood fast before the storm, lending my ears to who knows what. Perhaps I was hearing the final discordant notes of the great symphony of humanity, a sort of *cry before the end* . . . And as I was musing thus, this mad and monstrous apparition of a man desisted from his assault and limped away looking so *relieved* that I couldn't help feeling a little proud — as proud, I imagine, as a psychiatrist feels upon helping a patient with the dimmest prospects triumph over some refractory disorder.

Entrenched In Time

The lower our level of being, the more entrenched we are in time; and never has man been so entrenched in time as he is today, in this era of the *schedule*. For the ancient Indian there was no difference between a second and a century. A degraded type by comparison, the ancient Greek nevertheless displays a certain carelessness about time that redounds to his credit: unseduced by the idea of exact measurement, he is content to estimate the hour by the length of his shadow — in sharp contrast to the *clock-consciousness* of today. What once we invented now we kneel before, with servile respect. We are devotees of digits, dyed-in-the-wool watch-worshippers. The "watch": how aptly named, since our eyes are almost perpetually riveted to this object whose comparative tininess belies its extraordinary power — (what a theologian might term its *omnipotence.)* Like the faces of two lovers seated in opposite corners of a room, man's gaze and the clock's continually meet. Our every desire, move, and idea is dictated by time: *it* orders our life, and we consent to be so ordered, because one does not contradict the will of God — and time is the only god now acknowledged. Man's ever increasing vacancy as a spiritual and emotional being is a direct result of his idolatry of the clock and the calendar which, while they facilitate, encourage, and support material pursuits of every kind, leave the soul in darkness to shrivel up, and hinder the development of true feeling. Wisdom has no deadlines. Passion makes no appointments. So where would one expect to meet them in a society such as ours? That all clocks should be smashed to bits, all calendars burnt, all records of dates destroyed is probably too much to hope for. Man is likelier to remain what he is, what he has willingly become: a mere marionette of the Numeral.

The Perversion of Compassion

If compassion be understood according to its true Latin meaning, as *shared agony*, as the union of subject and object in a dance of corresponding dolor, there is no emotion more great among all the emotions that are — at least from the point of view of the man addicted to pain. But it is a perversion of compassion which has come into vogue and which prevails today. Men to whom agony is unknown have grabbed a hold of this concept and perverted it completely, reducing it to something low and effortless, when in fact compassion requires risk and supposes rank. We cannot have compassion with someone unless we are either his equal in trouble or *desire to be*. This is not merely a beautiful feeling that arises at sorrowful sights or a certificate of ethical superiority we may present to our peers, but a perilous undertaking, rooted either in the teeth-gnashing of traumatic experience or the nobility of sustained endeavor. Compassion is less a palliative for the object than a *trial* of the subject. Imposing a task on himself vis-à-vis universal pain, the compassionate man gallantly casts off the comforts of individuation. Every inferno he finds he stops off at, feverish to advance in suffering — to *improve* himself on the affective plane.

The Buddhist Hell

True Buddhism, we are told, has no truck with Hell; but the deviated version of this religion embraces Hell wholeheartedly. And it is a question whether we should concern ourselves with any but the deviated version of a religion, when that is the only one capable of making some kind of headway here on earth. The true version of a religion being neither practised nor even perceived save by a few fastidious seekers, what is the point of our playing around with it?

Scintillating as concepts like Sunyata, Maya, and Nirvana may be, let us not permit ourselves to fall under their spell. A mere handful of metaphysical tinsel — that is all they amount to. The main thing to keep in mind is that *no one* can resist Hell's delicious allure, least of all the Buddhists, who in their leisure have dreamt up a staggering ONE HUNDRED AND THIRTY-SIX places of punishment, all beautifully — and, need I add, maliciously — depicted in the central iconography of their paintings. When it comes to the invention and classification of tortures, the Far East is king. We Westerners and Middle Easterners have quite a bit to learn from these gory students of old Gautama. There are, it turns out, many terrible things which the One God — despite His marked penchant for the Terrible — neglected to teach us.

To get up such an impressive array of grim precincts as the Buddhists, you would have to have studied torture in detail and given it deep consideration. These virtuosos of vengeance can slice you and dice you in so many different ways you'll never *tire* of damnation. Christian and Muslim punishments are pathetic by comparison, and could only be expected to excite the amateur sadist. The devotees of Allah and Jehovah tried to be frightening, we must give them that much. Unfortunately, they failed. For all of their stunning feats of violence and conquest over the centuries, they just don't have what it takes to manufacture a *real Hell*. Stingy as it is, the Quran supplies us with a Hell of but seven divisions — just the sort of place a hardened sinner might visit on holiday. And Dante (a poet whose cosmic prowess is vastly over-rated) only succeeds in tacking on to this hopelessly feeble infernal mansion a couple of more stories.

One of the chief delusions of the West, caught up as it has been for so long in deeply satisfying pursuits like building, manufacturing, investing, buying, and selling is that Buddhists fail to appreciate the finer things of life — i.e., having a career — and don't understand what's most important — i.e., money — because they are dreamy, impractical souls, sunken in meditation. In fact they are anything but. It is *we* who are impractical and meditative by comparison. Let me tell you, building an inferno of the Buddhist scope demands great enterprise and even greater industry. Western man sets going a loop for the endless multiplication of roads, goods, gadgets, and machines, and thinks he's achieved something. He wants to be praised to the skies for his plumbing and air-conditioning, for his automobiles and light-bulbs. Well, let's just see him try his hand at *designing another world*. The Devil himself, as JudeaoChristianity conceives of him, could never succeed in the organization and direction of so vast a realm as the one which the Buddhists have so adeptly designed, prone as he is to be led astray by sophomoric pursuits like flirting with girls in gardens and playing practical jokes on scholars. Let's face it, the Orient has outdone Lucifer. It has put to shame our own personal Fiend on whom we have always so prided ourselves, imagining him quite fearsome indeed. And yet so bent are we on representing Eastern religion as more "enlightened" than our own, and so narrowly do we focus on the fine wisdom spouted by a few metaphysical athletes, that we completely lose sight of what *really matters,* and therefore deprive the East of that credit for ingenious cruelty which it so richly deserves.

Time and Vitality

Minutes, days, weeks, months: all of that means nothing.

If a man is alive, no clock or calendar he consults can tell him *his* time. Only in the land of the dead does time have one measurement. In the land of the dead clocks and calendars are like mirrors: they reflect your bloodless form back at you, confirming your total extinction.

Who are the dead? Those who can die no more. Who are the living? Those who die every day.

Only dead men bow before numbers. Only dead men confer objective reality on an arbitrary measurement and put themselves at the mercy of that measurement, making of it a reference, a rule, the form into which life fits and the guide which the will follows.

When you feel your blood, your muscles, your bones, your brain, when you feel the burning, the spasming, the pulsing, and the aching of your body, you recoil from clocks as if from a knife that wanted to cut the living essence out of you. For you, duration is a function of pain. Your nerves, scraped raw, have traversed seconds longer than centuries; and your heart has dragged itself, howling, through weeks longer than years. You know that age cannot be determined chronologically, but only emotionally, spiritually, and physiologically: it is not a question of how many days, but of how many *deaths*.

From Starlight to Electric Light

How we loathe the stars for having the boldness to hold aloof from the sphere we inhabit! Our pride is appalled by the distance they maintain: a distance which, were it possible, we would close by force. That business-savvy eye of ours which evaluates everything in terms of material profit now surveys with a mixture of aggression and disgust those potentially valuable jewels which stud the vault of heaven, and with extreme nostalgia we remember the time when, by dint of witchcraft, we managed to draw the stars down to earth — not, however (as historians of religion say) to worship them, but rather to *humiliate* them. We wanted to place those pretty and impertinent lights under our will, and so we did — for awhile. But soon enough they got wise to our tricks and stopped coming. Infuriated by this show of defiance, we vowed we would be avenged — and avenge ourselves we have, to a certain degree — and doubtless will, further. Were it in our power to pluck the stars from the sky and defile them as ferociously as we have the earth, we would do so in the blink of an eye, with a delight beyond words. If only we could command the movements of those sidereal rebels and assign them the positions *we* prefer! Or — even more desirably — drown them in the darkness of infinite space, forever blotting out the reproach they constitute. But knowing these to be transformations more desirable than possible, we have had to come up with a different way of asserting our dominance, of letting the universe know who's boss — and what we have done, in an attempt to demonstrate this, is to decorate every available horizon with these meaner, less dazzling lights that bow to our whims and shine at our behest. But, alas, unbeknownst to ourselves, we have failed even here. For, intending thus to display our power, we have only managed to make our impotence and fecklessness shine forth by dint of these wretched surrogates whose glow is neither beautiful nor celestial — lights that are *human, all too human* — lights *unworthy* of Heaven . . .

The Portioning Out of Eyes

The angel Mithra has ten thousand eyes; Ofaniel, eight thousand four hundred and sixty-six; and Azrael has as many eyes as there are men in the world. As for that seventy thousand-headed Angel whom Mohammed had the luck to meet in Heaven: even supposing him to be some kind of celestial Cyclops (a harp-playing Polyphemus who makes his home on a cloud rather than in a cave), he would still qualify as an ocular wonder. And, who knows, perhaps, in honor of St. Athanasius, God gave this angel three eyes per head, in which case he would possess the enviable privilege of being able to shed tears over two hundred ten thousand traumas at once. *Nota bene:* only to this band of beings immune to misfortune, to this "puissant host of glorious and happy spirits," as Barrow describes them, did God grant enough eyes to cry with. When it came man's turn, the Maker waxed parsimonious. For this forlornest and most afflicted of all creatures whose life is but a tissue of tortures and a series of incitements to sob without cease, for this toy of catastrophe and basket case of the creation, God could spare but two.

La Scienza Nuova

Poking around a bit in Biology's wardrobe, what did I come up with? Just what you'd expect: "Evolution," "Species," and other musty-smelling things. Come now, biologists: into the dustbin with all of this worn-out clothing! How very foolish and old-fashioned you look still going about in the same garb you wore a century ago! Rumor has it Darwin has all but done you in. I don't believe it though. By now I imagine you're sick to death of the *Origin*. So why not crack open, instead, a copy of the *Commedia?* Dante is your only hope. Who knows, maybe by reading him you can save Science from absolute ridicule. A Dantified science would see that what we are dealing with here are not "species" but circles of Hell, and that since increasing complexity of structure and feeling imply increasing pain and sensitivity to pain, beings do not progressively "evolve" but are progressively *damned*. A Dantified science would grasp the fact that life is Hell's *form*, and that what the old science so benignly — and benightedly — referred to as "organisms" are in fact styles of punishment, with man standing not at the peak of a biological process but at the bottom of an infernal pit.

The Unconquerable?

There is nothing in the world more terrifyingly determined than life, whose sworn purpose is to promote suffering. Not even the constant sabotage of her project by death manages to discourage her or to undermine her confidence. On the contrary, life's fanatical desire for conquest feeds off of death's opposition. A manmade catastrophe could wipe out every creature on the face of the earth, effectively putting an end to the scourge of reproduction, but it is doubtful if even then life would admit defeat. In fact she'd probably scarcely take notice. Who cannot envision her, one hundred years after this supreme devastation, creeping through some crack and comporting herself as if nothing at all had occurred?

About the Author

Christopher Spranger, the acclaimed author of *The Effort to Fall* (Green Integer, 1998) and *The Book of Tasks, Volume I: Atlantean Undertakings* (Coyote Arts, 2022) writes: "I was born March 29th, 1971, in Chicago, Illinois, and have been conspicuous ever since for my total failure to be a functioning part of the human species. I have not so much moved through life as slipped by alongside of it, like a fugitive. To ignore every goal reverenced by man: such has been my modus vivendi. I have no affiliations, no profession; there are no titles attached to my name; and I would even go so far as to say, at the risk of sounding excessive, that I am too unsynchronized with the material realm to have a terrestrial career. Who knows if at some time in the future my fleeting appearance upon the stage of this world might not be found classified among the forms of mirage?"

www.ingramcontent.com/pod-product-compliance
Lightning Source LLC
Chambersburg PA
CBHW070109080526
44586CB00013B/1241